DyslexiaGames.c

MW00934311

Practice Pages 2

A Unique Method of Writing Words, Symbols, Letters & Numbers

30 Worksheets

Writing Practice
For Kids Who Would
Rather be Climbing Trees.

The Thinking Tree

The Thinking TREE

www.DyslexiaGames.com

Dyslexia Games Series B –Book 3
Friendly Copyright Notice:

The Thinking Tree LLC   ●   29 S Main St   ●   Fortville, IN 46040   ●   info@dyslexiagames.com   ●   (317) 658-0850

Practice Pages

A Unique Method of Writing Symbols, Letters & Numbers. For Dyslexic Students.

By Sarah J. Brown & Anna Brown

Parent Teacher Instructions:

Provide the student with a pencil, eraser, and a fine point black pen.

The student will practice copying the letter, number or symbol in each row.
You may wish to show the child how to form the symbol before he does it on his
own. The child will draw the symbol in each of the empty spaces (little books).

These practice pages will be very helpful to children who tend to reverse and confuse
certain letters and numbers.

Pages 20 –30 are blank so that you can write in the letters or numbers that the child
needs more time to practice.

Practice Pages

Name:_____ **Date:**_____

1

Practice Pages

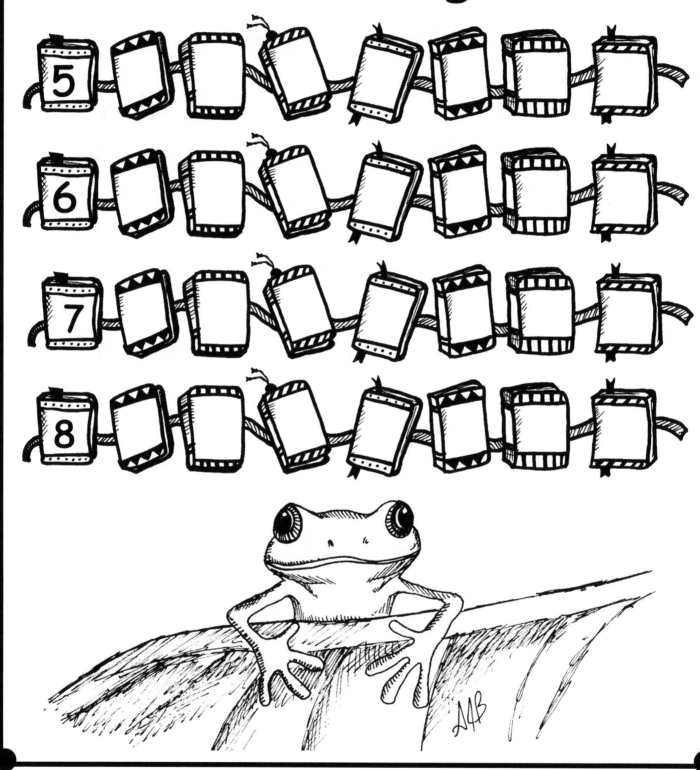

5
6
7
8

Name:_____ **Date:**_____

Practice Pages

Name: _____ **Date:** _____ 3

Practice Pages

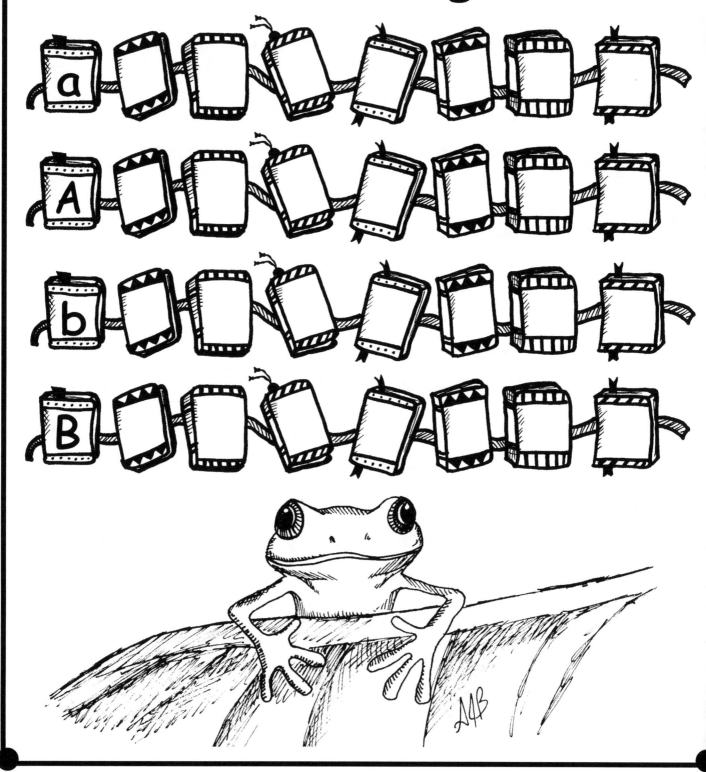

Name:_____ **Date:**_____

4

Practice Pages

Name: _____ **Date:** _____

5

Practice Pages

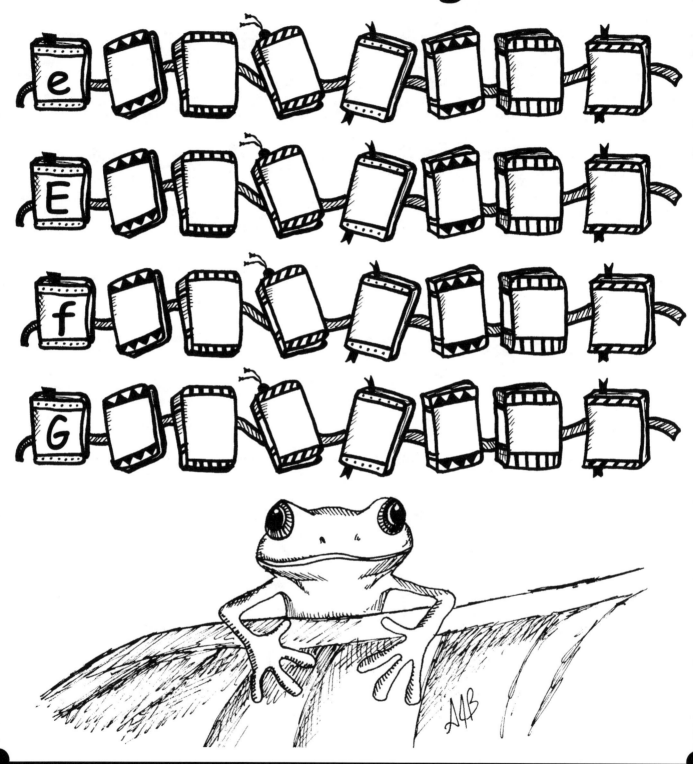

Practice Pages

Practice Pages

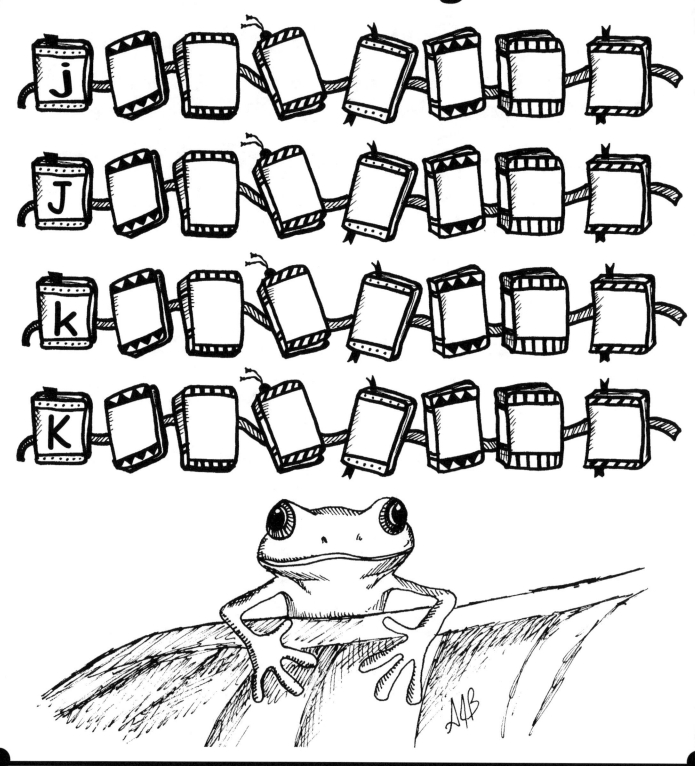

Name:_____ **Date:**_____

Practice Pages

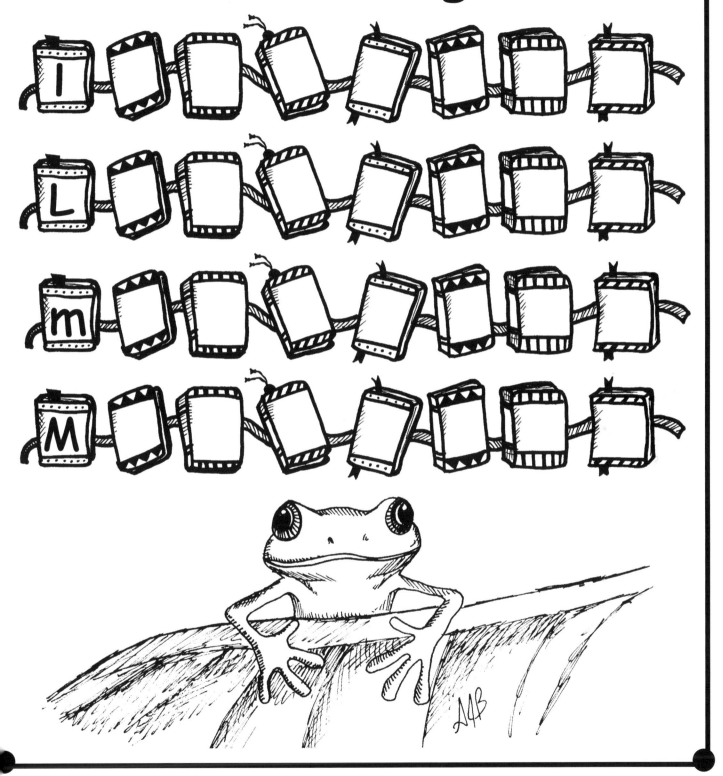

Practice Pages

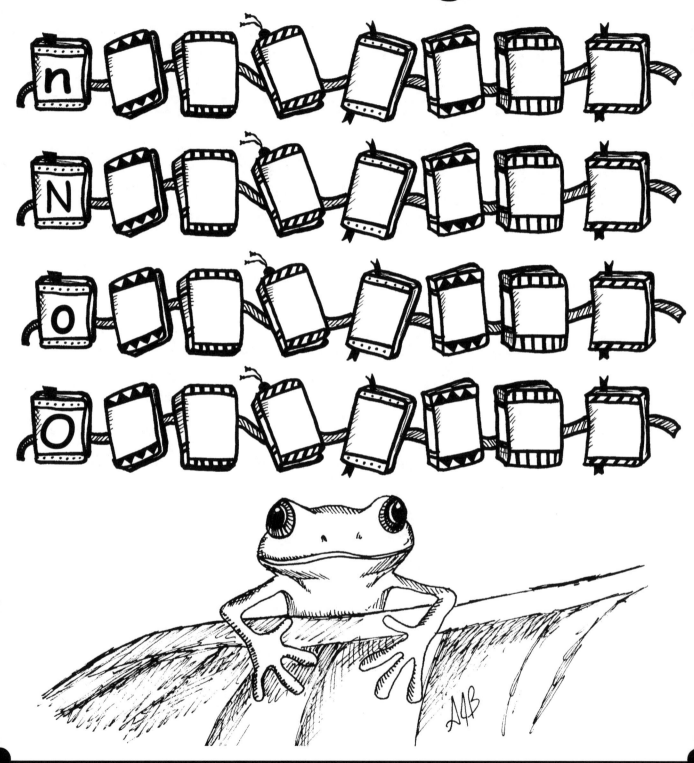

Name:_____ **Date:**_____

Practice Pages

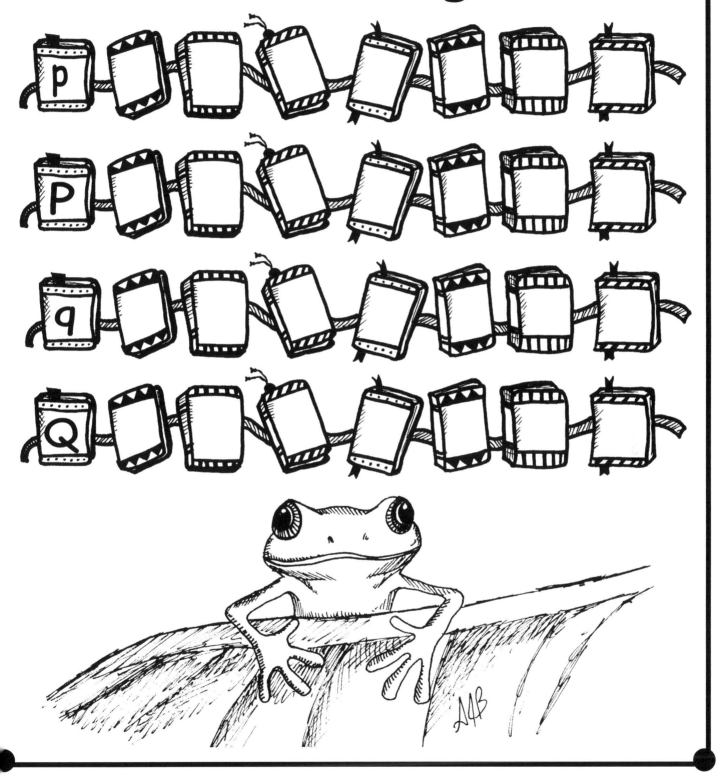

Practice Pages

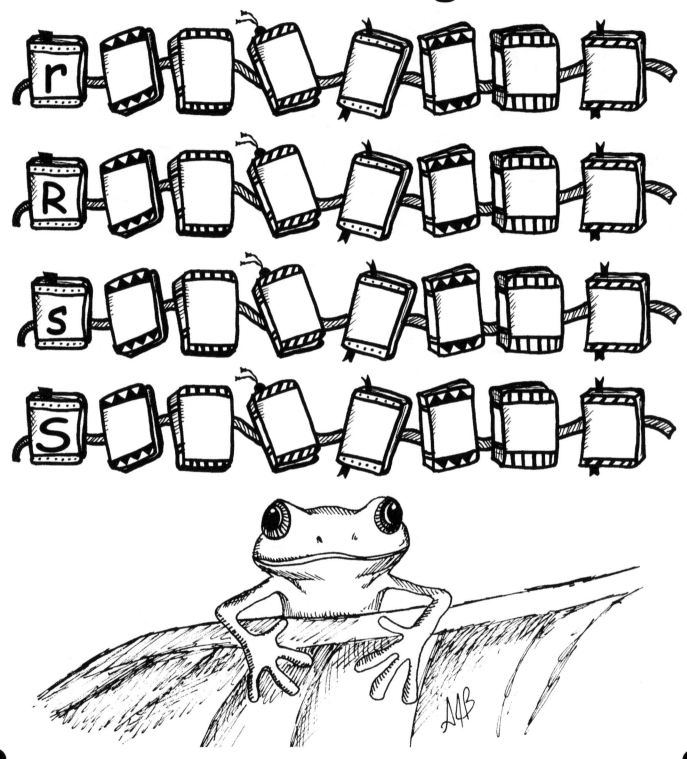

Name:_____   **Date:**_____

Practice Pages

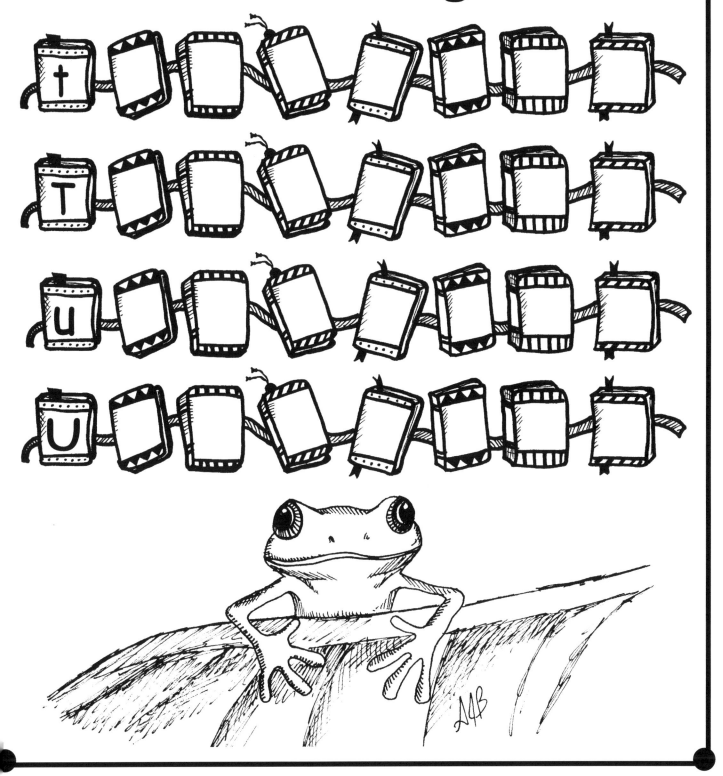

Practice Pages

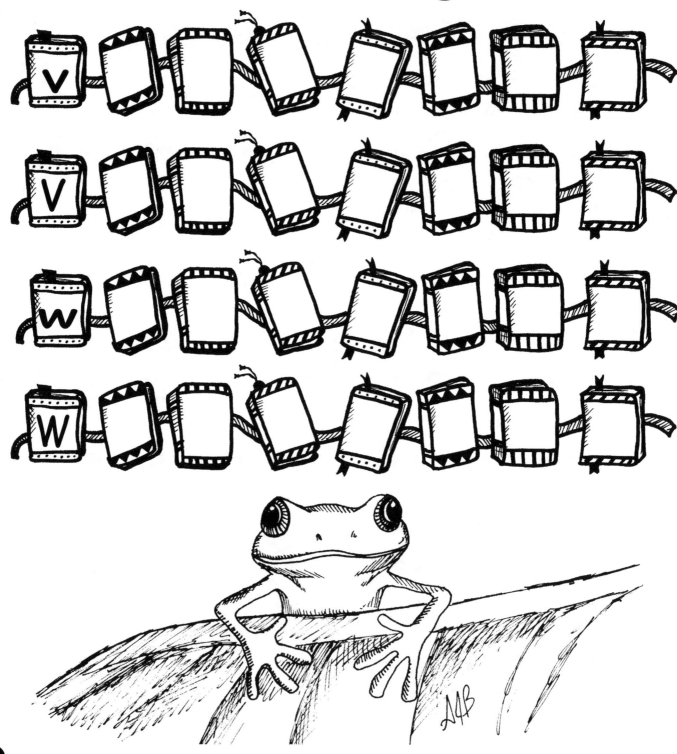

Name:_____ **Date:**_____

14

Practice Pages

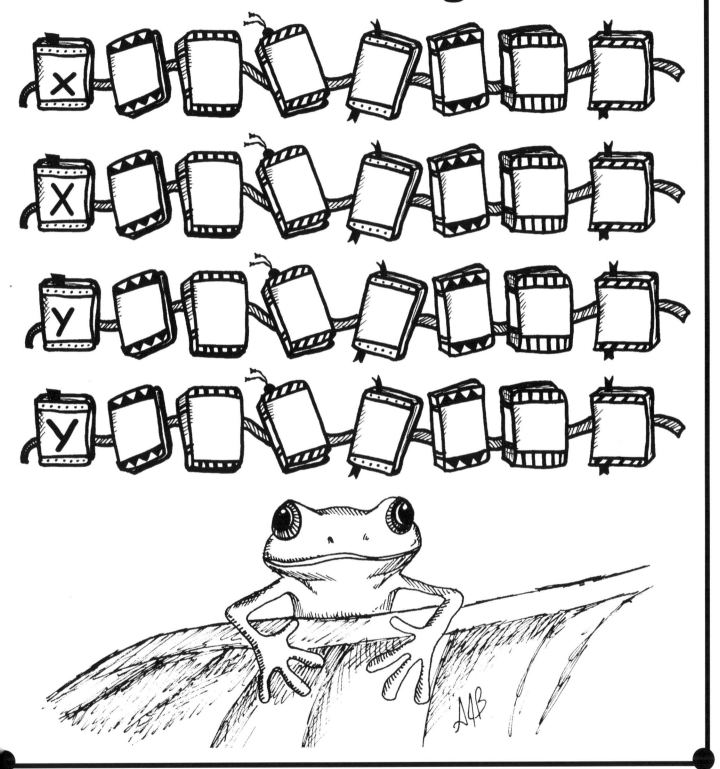

Practice Pages

Name:_____   **Date:**_____

Practice Pages

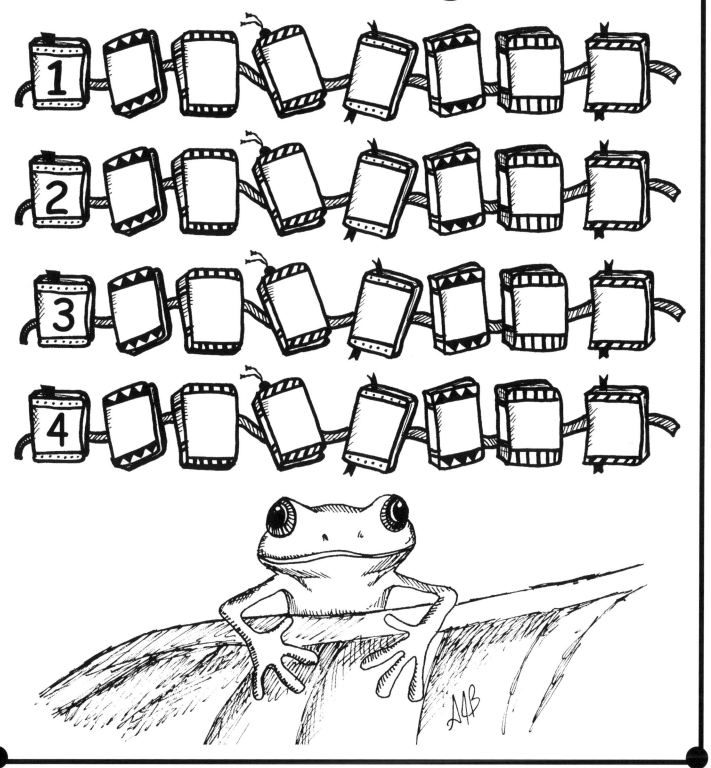

Name:_____ **Date:**_____

17

Practice Pages

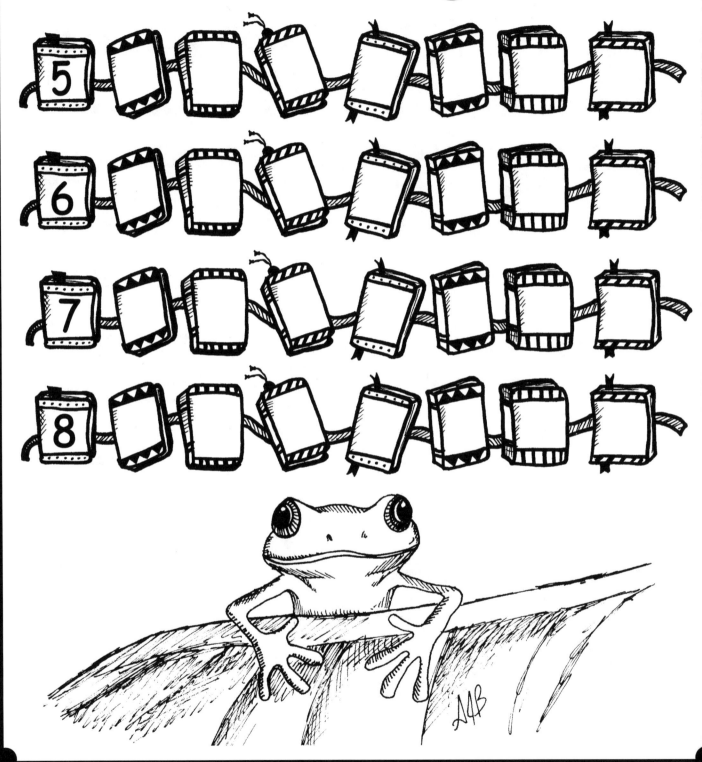

5

6

7

8

Name:_____ **Date:**_____

18

Practice Pages

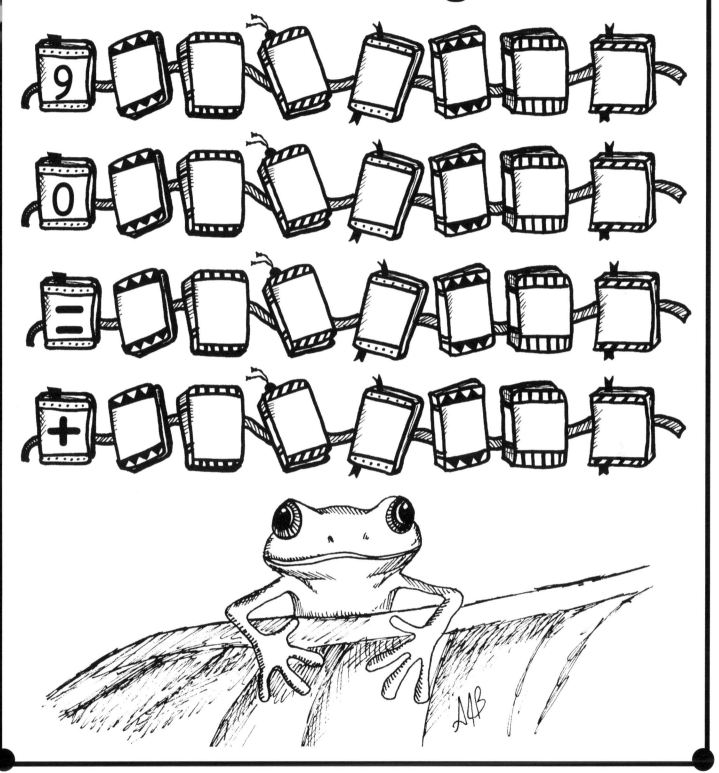

9

0

=

+

Practice Pages

Name:_____   Date:_____

Snail   Sn_ _ l   S _ _ _ l

Rooster   Roo_ _ _ r   R _ _ _ _ _ r

Turtle   Tu_ _ l_   T _ _ _ _ e

Goat   Go _ t   G _ _ t

Name:_____   **Date:**_____

21

Snail   Sn _ _ _   S _ _ _ _ _

Rooster   Roo _ _ _ _   R _ _ _ _ _ _

Turtle   Tu _ _ _ _   T _ _ _ _

Goat   Go _ _   G _ _ _

Toad T _ _ d T _ _ _ _ _ _ _

Tiger T _ g _ r T _ _ _ _ _ _ _ _ _

Bee B _ e B _ _ _ _ _ _ _ _

Hen H _ n H _ _ _ _ _ _ _ _

Toad   T___ ____ ____

Tiger   T____ ____ ____

Bee   B__ ___ __ __ ___

Hen   H__ ___ __ ___

T _ _ d T _ _ _ _ _ _ _ _ _ _ _

T _ _ _ r T _ _ _ _ _ _ _ _ _ _ _

B _ e B _ _ _ _ _ _ _ _ _ _ _

H _ n H _ _ _ _ _ _ _ _ _ _ _

Name: _____ **Date:** _____

25

Pet   P_t _e_ ___ ___

Shop S__p __o_ ____

Toy   T_y _o_ ___ ___

Store S___e _t___

Pet P_t ___ ___ ___

Shop S__p ____ ____

Toy T_y _o_ ___ ___

Store S___e _____

Pet _ _ t _ e _ _ _ _ _ _ _

Shop _ _ _ p _ _ o _ _ _ _ _

Toy _ _ y _ o _ _ _ _ _ _ _

Store _ _ o _ e S _ _ _ _

Name:_____ Date:_____

28

Cat food   c _ t f _ _ d _ a _ _ _ o _

Cat nip   c _ t n i _   _ _ t _ _ p

Cat food   c _ _ f _ o _ _ a _ f _ _ d

Cat nip   c _ _ n _ _   _ _ t _ _ p

Practice Pages

Certificate of Completion

_____

Name & Age

_____

Date of Completion

The Thinking TREE

_____

_____

Teacher

Made in the USA
Monee, IL
07 January 2025

72688688R00022